Francis Frith's
AROUND SHROPSHIRE

PHOTOGRAPHIC MEMORIES

Francis Frith's
AROUND SHROPSHIRE

◆

Dorothy Nicolle

FRITH BOOK Co

First published in the United Kingdom in 1999 by
Frith Book Company Ltd

Hardback Edition 1999
ISBN 1-85937-083-7

Paperback Edition 2001
ISBN 1-85937-326-7

British Library Cataloguing in Publication Data

Francis Frith's Shropshire
Dorothy Nicolle

Frith Book Company Ltd
Frith's Barn, Teffont,
Salisbury, Wiltshire SP3 5QP
Tel: +44 (0) 1722 716 376
Email: info@francisfrith.co.uk
www.francisfrith.co.uk

Printed and bound in Great Britain

AS WITH ANY HISTORICAL DATABASE THE FRITH ARCHIVE IS CONSTANTLY BEING CORRECTED AND IMPROVED
AND THE PUBLISHERS WOULD WELCOME INFORMATION ON OMISSIONS OR INACCURACIES

Contents

FRANCIS FRITH: *Victorian Pioneer*

FRANCIS FRITH, Victorian founder of the world-famous photographic archive, was a complex and multitudinous man. A devout Quaker and a highly successful Victorian businessman, he was both philosophic by nature and pioneering in outlook.

By 1855 Francis Frith had already established a wholesale grocery business in Liverpool, and sold it for the astonishing sum of £200,000, which is the equivalent today of over £15,000,000. Now a multi-millionaire, he was able to indulge his passion for travel. As a child he had pored over travel books written by early explorers, and his fancy and imagination had been stirred by family holidays to the sublime mountain regions of Wales and Scotland. 'What a land of spirit-stirring and enriching scenes and places!' he had written. He was to return to these scenes of grandeur in later years to 'recapture the thousands of vivid and tender memories', but with a different purpose. Now in his thirties, and captivated by the new science of photography, Frith

set out on a series of pioneering journeys to the Nile regions that occupied him from 1856 until 1860.

INTRIGUE AND ADVENTURE

He took with him on his travels a specially-designed wicker carriage that acted as both dark-room and sleeping chamber. These far-flung journeys were packed with intrigue and adventure. In his life story, written when he was sixty-three, Frith tells of being held captive by bandits, and of fighting 'an awful midnight battle to the very point of surrender with a deadly pack of hungry, wild dogs'. Sporting flowing Arab costume, Frith arrived at Akaba by camel seventy years before Lawrence, where he encountered 'desert princes and rival sheikhs, blazing with jewel-hilted swords'.

During these extraordinary adventures he was assiduously exploring the desert regions bordering the Nile and patiently recording the antiquities and peoples with his camera. He was the first photographer to venture beyond the sixth cataract. Africa was still the mysterious 'Dark Continent', and Stanley and Livingstone's historic meeting was a decade into the future. The conditions for picture taking confound belief. He laboured for hours in his wicker dark-room in the sweltering heat of the desert, while the volatile chemicals fizzed dangerously in their trays. Often he was forced to work in remote tombs and caves where conditions were cooler. Back in London he exhibited his photographs and was 'rapturously cheered' by members of the Royal Society. His reputation as a photographer was made overnight. An eminent modern historian has likened their impact on the population of the time to that on our own generation of the first photographs taken on the surface of the moon.

VENTURE OF A LIFE-TIME

Characteristically, Frith quickly spotted the opportunity to create a new business as a specialist publisher of photographs. He lived in an era of immense and sometimes violent change. For the poor in the early part of Victoria's reign work was a drudge and the hours long, and people had precious little free time to enjoy themselves.

Most had no transport other than a cart or gig at their disposal, and had not travelled far beyond the boundaries of their own town or village. However, by the 1870s, the railways had threaded their way across the country, and Bank Holidays and half-day Saturdays had been made obligatory by Act of Parliament. All of a sudden the ordinary working man and his family were able to enjoy days out and see a little more of the world.

With characteristic business acumen, Francis Frith foresaw that these new tourists would enjoy having souvenirs to commemorate their days out. In 1860 he married Mary Ann Rosling and set out with the intention of photographing every city, town and village in Britain. For the next thirty years he travelled the country by train and by pony and trap, producing fine photographs of seaside resorts and beauty spots that were keenly bought by millions of Victorians. These prints were painstakingly pasted into family albums and pored over during the dark nights of winter, rekindling precious memories of summer excursions.

THE RISE OF FRITH & CO

Frith's studio was soon supplying retail shops all over the country. To meet the demand he gathered about him a small team of photographers, and published the work of independent artist-photographers of the calibre of Roger Fenton and Francis Bedford. In order to gain some understanding of the scale of Frith's business one only has to look at the catalogue issued by Frith & Co in 1886: it runs to some 670

court card, but there was little room for illustration. In 1899, a year after Frith's death, a new card measuring 5.5 x 3.5 inches became the standard format, but it was not until 1902 that the divided back came into being, with address and message on one face and a full-size illustration on the other. *Frith & Co* were in the vanguard of postcard development, and Frith's sons Eustace and Cyril continued their father's monumental task, expanding the number of views offered to the public and recording more and more places in Britain, as the coasts and countryside were opened up to mass travel.

Francis Frith died in 1898 at his villa in Cannes, his great project still growing. The archive he created continued in business for another seventy years. By 1970 it contained over a third of a million pictures of 7,000 cities, towns and villages. The massive photographic record Frith has left to us stands as a living monument to a special and very remarkable man.

pages, listing not only many thousands of views of the British Isles but also many photographs of most European countries, and China, Japan, the USA and Canada – note the sample page shown above from the hand-written *Frith & Co* ledgers detailing pictures taken. By 1890 Frith had created the greatest specialist photographic publishing company in the world, with over 2,000 outlets – more than the combined number that Boots and WH Smith have today! The picture on the right shows the *Frith & Co* display board at Ingleton in the Yorkshire Dales. Beautifully constructed with mahogany frame and gilt inserts, it could display up to a dozen local scenes.

POSTCARD BONANZA

The ever-popular holiday postcard we know today took many years to develop. In 1870 the Post Office issued the first plain cards, with a pre-printed stamp on one face. In 1894 they allowed other publishers' cards to be sent through the mail with an attached adhesive halfpenny stamp. Demand grew rapidly, and in 1895 a new size of postcard was permitted called the

Frith's Archive: *A Unique Legacy*

FRANCIS FRITH'S legacy to us today is of immense significance and value, for the magnificent archive of evocative photographs he created provides a unique record of change in 7,000 cities, towns and villages throughout Britain over a century and more. Frith and his fellow studio photographers revisited locations many times down the years to update their views, compiling for us an enthralling and colourful pageant of British life and character.

We tend to think of Frith's sepia views of Britain as nostalgic, for most of us use them to conjure up memories of places in our own lives with which we have family associations. It often makes us forget that to Francis Frith they were records of daily life as it was actually being lived in the cities, towns and villages of his day. The Victorian age was one of great and often bewildering change for ordinary people, and though the pictures evoke an impression of slower times, life was as busy and hectic as it is today.

We are fortunate that Frith was a photographer of the people, dedicated to recording the minutiae of everyday life. For it is this sheer wealth of visual data, the painstaking chronicle of changes in dress, transport, street layouts, buildings, housing, engineering and landscape that captivates us so much today. His remarkable images offer us a powerful link with the past and with the lives of our ancestors.

TODAY'S TECHNOLOGY

Computers have now made it possible for Frith's many thousands of images to be accessed almost instantly. In the Frith archive today, each photograph is carefully 'digitised' then stored on a CD Rom. Frith archivists can locate a single photograph amongst thousands within seconds. Views can be catalogued and sorted under a variety of categories of place and content to the immediate benefit of researchers. Inexpensive reference prints can be created for them at the touch of a mouse button, and a wide range of books and other printed materials assembled and published for a wider, more general readership - in the next twelve months over a hundred Frith local history titles will be published! The

See Frith at www. francisfrith.co.uk

day-to-day workings of the archive are very different from how they were in Francis Frith's time: imagine the herculean task of sorting through eleven tons of glass negatives as Frith had to do to locate a particular sequence of pictures! Yet the archive still prides itself on maintaining the same high standards of excellence laid down by Francis Frith, including the painstaking cataloguing and indexing of every view.

It is curious to reflect on how the internet now allows researchers in America and elsewhere greater instant access to the archive than Frith himself ever enjoyed. Many thousands of individual views can be called up on screen within seconds on one of the Frith internet sites, enabling people living continents away to revisit the streets of their ancestral home town, or view places in Britain where they have enjoyed holidays. Many overseas researchers welcome the chance to view special theme selections, such as transport, sports, costume and ancient monuments.

We are certain that Francis Frith would have heartily approved of these modern developments, for he himself was always working at the very limits of Victorian photographic technology.

THE VALUE OF THE ARCHIVE TODAY

Because of the benefits brought by the computer, Frith's images are increasingly studied by social historians, by researchers into genealogy and ancestory, by architects, town planners, and by teachers and schoolchildren involved in local history projects. In addition, the archive offers every one of

us a unique opportunity to examine the places where we and our families have lived and worked down the years. Immensely successful in Frith's own era, the archive is now, a century and more on, entering a new phase of popularity.

THE PAST IN TUNE WITH THE FUTURE

Historians consider the Francis Frith Collection to be of prime national importance. It is the only archive of its kind remaining in private ownership and has been valued at a million pounds. However, this figure is now rapidly increasing as digital technology enables more and more people around the world to enjoy its benefits.

Francis Frith's archive is now housed in an historic timber barn in the beautiful village of Teffont in Wiltshire. Its founder would not recognize the archive office as it is today. In place of the many thousands of dusty boxes containing glass plate negatives and an all-pervading odour of photographic chemicals, there are now ranks of computer screens. He would be amazed to watch his images travelling round the world at unimaginable speeds through network and internet lines.

The archive's future is both bright and exciting. Francis Frith, with his unshakeable belief in making photographs available to the greatest number of people, would undoubtedly approve of what is being done today with his lifetime's work. His photographs, depicting our shared past, are now bringing pleasure and enlightenment to millions around the world a century and more after his death.

SHROPSHIRE – *An Introduction*

SHROPSHIRE PEOPLE have a saying: God practised on Paradise and only then did He make Shropshire. Many people in Britain are unaware that Shropshire exists at all. If they do know the county, it is often because they have passed through it on their way to somewhere else. But for those of us lucky enough to have discovered it, and I speak as one such person, it is certainly a little bit of Heaven.

However, there must have been times in the past, particularly in the 18th and 19th centuries, when large areas of the county seemed more akin to Hell than to Heaven. But even then, away from the smoke and grime of the industrial revolution, parts of the county will still have been remarkably beautiful and peaceful.

Shropshire has always been a county of contrasts. It sits on the Marches (or borders) with Wales, and the land here has been fought over from Dark Age times. King Offa in the late 8th century built his famous dyke through here in order to try and draw a line of demarcation between the two nations - not that it worked.

With the arrival of the Normans the county became vitally important as a military stronghold. This was not only to protect the borders but also to control the newly subject people. Local legends still talk of Wild Edric, who rose in revolt against the Normans in the 1080s and lies buried in the old Roman lead mines of the Stiperstones ready to rise once more when we have an English monarch on the throne. He has been waiting a long time!

The following centuries were to see an enormous rise in the wealth of the area along with the growing importance of the wool trade to the country's economy. Wool from all over northern and central Wales, as well as from the hills of Shropshire, came into the county's towns, was bought by the merchants and shipped down the Severn to Bristol and on to Europe. The wool merchants were the wealthiest and most powerful commoners in medieval England; among these Nicholas de Ludlow and his son, Lawrence, were supreme.

Evidence of the wealth of these merchants (and the later drapers, the merchants who dealt in woollen cloth) is to be seen all over the county. Stokesay Castle, for example, was just one of several homes owned by Lawrence de Ludlow at the end of the 13th century By the time of the 16th century the cloth trade was the source of the wealth of many magnificent town houses, particularly in Shrewsbury, where the flamboyant use of timber and the elaborate carving, not to mention the very size of some of the buildings, shows off this wealth.

During the 16th century, too, the general wealth of England increased. It was not just the nobility who benefited. This wealth trickled down through the classes, even if it never did quite reach those at the bottom of the

an event took place in Shropshire that was to change the whole world. Abraham Darby, an ironmaster, started to carry out experiments in how to smelt iron using coke. For centuries iron had been smelted using charcoal; this was not only wasteful of resources, but it meant that only small quantities of iron could be smelted at any one time. Darby was not alone in working on this problem, but it was he who finally mastered the technique and thus ushered in the modern industrial world.

social pile. As a result, we see more and more houses being built throughout the country at this time: this is true of Shropshire too.

Then the country was split by the Civil War. Generally the people of Shropshire supported the Royalist cause, but as in any civil war, towns and families were often split in their allegiances. Today Shrewsbury still has its 'Traitor's Gate' - did the town fall as a result of a traitor letting the Roundheads in? We will never know for sure. Several of the county's castles were destroyed at this time - today Bridgnorth's castle leans at an alarming angle as a result of being blown up by Roundheads.

But it was in the next century, in 1709, that

For the next one hundred years Shropshire was at the heart of technological development, the 'Silicon Valley' of its day. The greatest innovators of the time came here to study what was being done - people like Richard Trevithick who invented the first steam locomotive, 'Ironmad' John Wilkinson and Thomas Telford. Many went home and worked on their ideas elsewhere, and thus the new technology spread. By the end of the 1800s Ironbridge was in decline; today the area is largely made up of museums - a World Heritage Site.

The county's capital is Shrewsbury. We know little about the town's early history, and today we cannot even seem to determine how to pronounce its name. Is it Shrowsbury or Shrewsbury? What does it even mean? The 'bury' element is easy - that tells us that the early Saxon settlement on this site was fortified in some way. But who or what was 'Scrobb', as the first element is spelt in early documents? Some would have it that the name means 'the fortified place with the shrubs'. This explanation runs counter to most Saxon place names where usually the first element is either a distinguishing feature about the place (what, after all, is different about a few shrubs?) or a person's name. I favour the explanation that there was a person called Scrobb who settled here with his people and set about defending his homestead.

And its pronunciation? One has to assume that early clerics tried to spell phonetically whatever they thought they heard. This would imply that the early pronunciation was closer to Shrowsbury than Shrewsbury. How did it come to change? Local tradition has it that once upon a time a mapmaker made a

spelling mistake, and from that day to this people have argued over how the town's name should be pronounced!

Interestingly, Shrewsbury is still only a town, although in recent years it has applied several times to receive city status. The town was first offered city status during the 16th century, but refused it then. Local people said that they preferred to be the most important town in the country rather than a second- or third-rate city. It is a sentiment with which I rather agree. As a town, Shrewsbury must be unrivalled in the country with one or two unusual claims to fame. For example, it can be described as the 'most haunted town (not city!) in England'. Also, it has been described as the politest town in England - rather a welcoming accolade, I think you will agree.

For a long time the second most important town in Shropshire was Bridgnorth to the east. Also situated on a good, defendable site, it benefited from being further downstream on the River Severn and so could continue to trade for a much longer period each year than Shrewsbury. (In Shrewsbury the river was

often impassable for months at a time in periods of drought.) Not only was there river traffic going through Bridgnorth but, as the town's name tells us, there was also a bridge crossing point over the Severn here so that road traffic benefited too.

Unfortunately for Bridgnorth, this advantage over so many other local towns was lost the moment that the canals were built. Traders who in the past had always travelled to Bridgnorth to get their goods onto the Severn could now reach their markets directly by canal.

From the 1500s Ludlow, in the south of Shropshire, began to rival Bridgnorth as the county's second town. Much, much earlier, from Norman times, this town with its castle had been developed primarily to control the Marches region. To begin with, Ludlow had just been one in a series of castles all along the border. However, its almost central position in the Marches meant that before long it became the most important of all the border castles.

Ludlow's importance was to increase enormously in 1485 when Henry Tudor grabbed the crown after the Battle of Bosworth and became Henry VII, King of England and Wales: two countries were now under one ruler who was based in London. Problems quickly arose over the administration of Wales from so far away, and so it was decided to administer the Principality from the border town of Ludlow, in Shropshire.

This meant that Ludlow became, in some ways, more important than Shrewsbury. For the next two hundred years and more Ludlow thrived. It became a very genteel place in which to live, and this is reflected in many of the buildings of the town. Even today the town still has this aura of style and sophistication and, with its annual festival each July and the Michelin stars of its restaurants, the town continues to attract the more discerning visitor.

Shrewsbury, Bridgnorth, Ludlow, the market towns of Oswestry and Newport, Market Drayton and Church Stretton, Bishop's Castle and Whitchurch - today all of these towns have been overtaken by the new town of Telford established in the 1960s. This town, named for Thomas Telford who was County Surveyor in Shropshire for nearly 50 years, is made up of numerous smaller towns, villages and hamlets, and its population will soon probably equal that of all the other main towns in the county. Telford was planned to act primarily as a dormitory town for the Birmingham area, but investment here has been such that it has expanded at an enormous rate and is now an industrial centre in its own right.

Despite this growth, when people outside of Shropshire think of the county (if they ever do!) they imagine a place that is still very rural and dotted with small market towns. This, indeed, is true. Unfortunately, Shropshire's traditional dependence on 'farming industries' has meant that it has suffered considerably in recent years as that same industry has declined and struggles to survive.

Other industries have arrived instead - notably the light industries in and around the new town of Telford. But at the end of the day much of the county seems to be falling back on that standby industry - tourism.

Shropshire certainly has much to offer the tourist - a wealth of wonderful historic sites from all periods of our history, set in countryside that is spectacularly beautiful. It has been said of Shropshire, however, that there are within the county 'no buildings worthy of note'. Indeed, there are no magnificent palaces, cathedrals and the like. Our gems may be small, but they are still gems for all that - the timber-framed buildings have a charm and character all their own, with their delightful carvings and their wriggling rooflines. Also, the very inaccessibility of much of the countryside has meant that, for example many small churches have survived almost untouched.

Finally, the beauty of the county has inspired many writers. Today one thinks particularly of Edith Pargeter (often better known as Ellis Peters, creator of the fictional detective Brother Cadfael) who set so many of her novels here. Another writer who will always be associated with the county is AE Housman. Although he was born and always lived outside Shropshire, his volume of poetry, 'The Shropshire Lad', was to inspire many soldiers during the First World War. There are many others too - from William Langland in the 14th century to Mary Webb, whose descriptions of the Shropshire countryside one hundred years ago cannot be equalled.

One thing unites all these writers from so many different times and lifestyles. That is their undiluted love of Shropshire. I hope that as you browse though the pictures in this volume you will come to see why they felt so strongly about the county, if you do not understand already.

WROXETER, THE RUINED BATHHOUSE c1864 2188

Wroxeter was the fourth largest town in Roman Britain. Today little remains above ground level. The photograph shows the hypocaust heating system for the bathhouse in the foreground and, behind it, the 'Old Work' - the tallest chunk of Roman masonry surviving anywhere in the country.

SHREWSBURY, THE ENGLISH BRIDGE 1931 83873

The town is almost completely surrounded by the River Severn, so that most visitors to Shrewsbury enter it over one of its bridges. The English Bridge was built in 1774 by John Gwynne. Originally much steeper, it was levelled off and widened in the 1920s to allow easier passage for modern traffic.

SHREWSBURY, THE NAG'S HEAD 1891 28910
Everyone seems to be posing for the
photographer in this picture. Notice
particularly the lad on the right taking down
the shutters from the shop window. Inns called
the Nag's Head were originally places where
horses could be hired, although I doubt if this
was still happening in the 1890s.

SHREWSBURY, THE UNICORN HOTEL 1891 28911

The Unicorn Hotel has long disappeared, but the timber building with the gable ends is still here - it is now a wine merchants, and parts of the shop have hardly changed with time. In fact the interior was used as a set for Ebeneezer Scrooge's office during the recent filming of Dickens' 'A Christmas Carol'.

SHREWSBURY, WYLE COP 1896 38099a

This part of Shrewsbury suffered a great fire in the 1390s, and so these buildings date from the 1400s. The building on the right has a particularly decorative window which is original. The inscription below records a visit by Henry Tudor in 1485 when on his way to victory at the Battle of Bosworth.

SHREWSBURY, THE OLD MARKET HALL AND PRINCESS STREET 1911 63226

Once named Candle Lane because candles were sold here, the street was renamed to commemorate the visit of Princess Victoria in the 1800s. The market hall dates from the reign of Queen Elizabeth I, and was used as a corn and produce market on the ground floor and a cloth market upstairs.

SHREWSBURY, HIGH STREET 1911 63228

The wonderful timber buildings here all date from the late 1500s. They were built by wealthy cloth merchants, or drapers, and so it seems appropriate that one shop, R Maddox & Co, is still selling cloth and children's dresses.

SHREWSBURY, HIGH STREET 1931 83877
The same scene twenty years later - and just the traffic has changed. Apart from the building at the end of the street, which has been replaced by an award-winning 1960s monstrosity, all these buildings are still there.

SHREWSBURY, MILK STREET 1911 63227
Many street names were derived from the products traded in them. Here milk and dairy products were sold.
Other similar local names are Fish Street and Butcher Row. Sometimes names changed. Who would want to live
in Swine Street, no matter how smart the houses? It therefore changed to St John's Hill - much more elegant.

SHREWSBURY, BUTCHER ROW 1924 76179

SHREWSBURY
Butcher Row 1924
The timbers in the Abbot's House, as this building is known, have recently been dated - the trees were cut down in 1457. The ground floor served as a row of individual butcher's booths - it is just possible to make out the meat hooks above the two windows on the left.

◆

SHREWSBURY
The Old Mint 1891
So called because a moneyer is reputed to have stayed here for a time in the 14th century, this is really part of a medieval merchant's house. Today, parts of the old building (the arched doorway for example) can still be seen incorporated into the interior decor of a shop on Pride Hill.

SHREWSBURY, THE OLD MINT 1891 28924

SHREWSBURY, PRIDE HILL 1931 83881

Today Pride Hill is a pedestrianised area. The buildings on the right are much the same, although Woolworth's has been removed to make way for the entrance to a multi-storey shopping centre called the Darwin Centre. It is named for Charles Darwin, who was born in Shrewsbury in 1809.

SHREWSBURY, THE RAVEN HOTEL AND CASTLE STREET 1911 63223

Now demolished, the Raven Hotel had many famous visitors in its time. George Farquhar stayed here while writing his play 'The Recruiting Officer'. Jenny Lind, the Swedish Nightingale, stayed here. So too did William Palmer, the Rugeley Poisoner, who began to poison his last victim, John Cook, while they both stayed here.

SHREWSBURY, FRANKWELL 1911 63256

This building still exists - but not in Shropshire. It was an inn known as The String of Horses; it now sits in the Avoncroft Museum of Buildings at Bromsgrove, having been removed in the 1960s to make way for a roundabout.

SHREWSBURY, THE BOAT HOUSE 1911 63218

Today there is a footbridge crossing the River Severn near this point. Notice how the ferryman is pulling on the rope to take his passengers across the river. Each of his passengers will have paid ½d for the ride. The ferry was replaced by the footbridge in 1923.

SHREWSBURY, ABBEY FOREGATE 1896 38100

Abbey Foregate was the main road to London. By the time this photograph was taken most people would have travelled there by train. In the days of the stagecoach, however, the journey could take sixteen hours in the 'Wonder', the fastest coach in England.

HAUGHMOND HILL 1891 28955

This castle, since demolished, sits on Queen Eleanor's Bower. Legend says that she watched her husband win the Battle of Shrewsbury from here in 1403. Henry IV won that battle. He was married twice, but neither lady was called Eleanor. As is the way with legends, one story has obviously become muddled with another.

HAUGHMOND ABBEY
The Chapter House 1891

This was an Augustinian abbey founded in 1135 by William Fitz Alan. The Fitz Alans were powerful Shropshire landowners; the family was later to inherit Arundel (where the family is still based) in 1243. From William both the Stuart royal line in Scotland and the English line of the Earls of Norfolk descend.

◆

ATCHAM
The Bridge and Church 1891

Fortunately, although a new road bridge has replaced this one, the old bridge survives as a footbridge. The church is dedicated to St Eata, a 7th-century missionary who settled here to convert the pagan Anglo-Saxons. The church was later built using stone robbed from nearby Wroxeter.

HAUGHMOND ABBEY, THE CHAPTER HOUSE 1891 28957

ATCHAM, THE BRIDGE AND CHURCH 1891 28958

MUCH WENLOCK, THE GASKELL ARMS 1911 63261
The American author Henry James visited here
in 1877. He described Wenlock as an 'ancient
little town . . . with no great din of vehicles . . . a
dozen 'publics' (pubs), with tidy whitewashed
cottages . . . and little girls bobbing curtsies in
the street'.

MUCH WENLOCK, THE RAILWAY STATION 1903 50277

The railway line disappeared in the 1960s, and today the station is a private house. 'Wenlock' is thought by some to mean 'white church' in the old Celtic tongue, which would imply that there was a Christian settlement here from very early times indeed.

MUCH WENLOCK, HIGH STREET 1911 63266

Sometimes things don't change - the baker's shop on the left is still selling bread and cakes. The large house on the right is supposedly haunted by two children playing with a spinning top on the balcony. Although the facade has a date in the 1680s, internal timbers in this building date from the 1400s.

MUCH WENLOCK, SHINETON STREET **1936** 87402

MUCH WENLOCK
Shineton Street 1936
It was here in the mid 1800s that Dr William Penny Brookes practised. He had the unusual idea that exercise was good for people and founded the annual Wenlock Olympic Games to encourage his patients to take up sport. This idea was later copied by Baron de Coubertin, who began the international Olympic movement.

◆

PITCHFORD HALL **1891**
Undoubtedly the finest surviving timber-framed mansion in Shropshire, this was built in the 1500s by a wealthy wool merchant called Adam Otley. In the grounds of the house there is also a timber-framed tree-house that Queen Victoria played in as a child.

PITCHFORD HALL **1891** 28961

COUND, THE VILLAGE c1955 C718006

As a village Cound spreads itself over a large area. Its inn sits about a mile away looking out over the River
Severn with its back to the road - in fact, it was originally built to serve boatmen travelling along the river, but no-
one comes that way now.

COUND, COUND HALL c1955 C718007

Built in 1704, this fine mansion is especially famous for its superb staircase which is described as 'flying' up the
back wall. The building has for a long time been abandoned and left to fall into a ruinous state, but fortunately
plans are now being made to restore it.

CHURCH STRETTON
The Sandford Hotel 1910
By the mid 1800s Church Stretton had become a holiday resort for people keen on country walking, and many hotels were established to serve this market. On the side of the hills of the Long Mynd houses crowded at all levels, giving rise to the area's nickname of 'Little Switzerland'.

◆

CHURCH STRETTON
Burway Road 1910
Here we see evidence of early tourism in the area with a wonderful display of post-cards in the shop on the right. The sign to the left of the picture advertises 'Cycles for Hire' - why anyone would want to ride up the Burway I do not know - it is the steepest road in the county.

CHURCH STRETTON, THE SANDFORD HOTEL 1910 62722

CHURCH STRETTON, BURWAY ROAD 1910 62717

CHURCH STRETTON, HIGH STREET 1910 62719
A delightful gravestone survives in the town's churchyard commemorating Ann Cook who died in 1814: 'On a Thursday she was born, On a Thursday made a bride, On a Thursday broke her leg, And on a Thursday died'.

CHURCH STRETTON, HIGH STREET 1910 62721
The town sits beside a Roman road across which is the hill of Caer Caradoc. Somewhere in Shropshire the Celtic hero, Caractacus, fought and was defeated by the invading Romans before fleeing north where he was later captured. Did the battle take place here, on the hill that bears his name?

ALL STRETTON, THE LONG MYND HILLS 1910 62742
Nearby is the Cwm Spring supplying mineral water which is bottled in the village Until recently, local
householders even used the water for bathing. Villagers can still get free mineral water from a tap by the
entrance to the bottling plant.

**OSWESTRY, SMITHFIELD CATTLE MARKET
c1955** O63042
Sitting right on the English/Welsh border,
Oswestry has always served as a market
centre for a wide area extending well into
central Wales. Even today, the Welsh
language can sometimes be heard here.

OSWESTRY, CHURCH STREET 1962 O63108

Oswestry was the site of the Battle of Maserfeld in AD 641. King Oswald of Northumbria was killed, his body cut into pieces and the pieces hung in a tree - hence Oswald's tree or Oswestry.

OSWESTRY, CHURCH STREET c1965 O63106

Wilfred Owen, who must rank as one of Britain's finest war poets, was born in Oswestry in 1893. He was later to die in the very last days of the First World War. Among his best known poems are 'Strange Meeting' and 'Dulce et Decorum Est'.

OSWESTRY, LLWYD'S MANSION 1957 O63056

OSWESTRY
Llwyd's Mansion 1957
The town has suffered a great deal over the centuries: it was regularly ransacked and burnt - sometimes by the Welsh, sometimes by the English. There are therefore only a few really old buildings. Llwyd's Mansion dates from 1604.

◆

GOBOWEN
Preeshenlle Chapel c1960
Today Gobowen is famous for its Italianate style railway station. The station was decommissioned by British Rail and was saved and restored by the children and teachers of the local school, who still continue to run the ticket office as part of their 'work experience'.

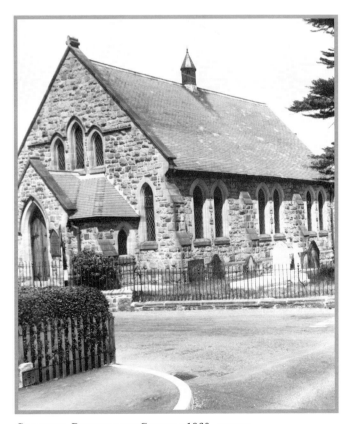

GOBOWEN, PREESHENLLE CHAPEL c1960 G234020

WESTON RHYN, THE VILLAGE AND THE POST OFFICE c1955 W567001

WESTON RHYN
The Village and the Post Office c1955
Just outside the village of Weston Rhyn there is an unusual folly - a romanticised Stonehenge. It was erected in the 19th century by Thomas Barnes. He had previously made his fortune as a cotton mill owner and by investing in the railways.

ELLESMERE
Scotland Street c1955
Despite its name, Scotland Street actually leads to Wales. Ellesmere was once part of the dowry of King John's illegitimate daughter, Joan. She was married to Llewellyn, Prince of Gwynedd, in 1205 and subsequently acted as intermediary between Llewellyn in Wales and her father (and later her brother, Henry III) in England.

ELLESMERE, SCOTLAND STREET c1955 E180061

ELLESMERE, SCOTLAND STREET c1960 E180085
Here we see the same street five years later and seen from the other direction. Notice that the porch at the entrance to the Black Lion Hotel has disappeared.

WHITCHURCH, HIGH STREET 1901 47183
Whitchurch must be one of Shropshire's oldest towns. In Roman times it was known as Mediolanum, and was an important fort and posting station on the road linking Wroxeter and Chester. The High Street still follows the old Roman road through the centre of the town.

HAWKSTONE PARK, GIANT'S WELL 1898 42220

HAWKSTONE PARK
Giant's Well 1898
Was this the original theme park? The grounds here were laid out in the 1700s with all sorts of follies - a shell-lined grotto, a ruined castle, a rickety bridge over a narrow chasm, even a resident hermit. Today, having been restored, the park is once again open to the public every summer.

◆

WESTON UNDER REDCASTLE
The Hawkstone Park Hotel c1955
Many people came to Hawkstone to visit the follies - apparently it was particularly popular with honeymooners in Victorian times. The hotel was built to accommodate these visitors.

WESTON UNDER REDCASTLE, THE HAWKSTONE PARK HOTEL c1955 W559014

WESTON UNDER REDCASTLE, HAWKSTONE HALL MONASTERY C1955 W559027
Today the hall is a centre and retreat for missionaries from around the world. In the late 18th century it was the home of Rowland Hill, who became famous as a general in Wellington's army in the Peninsular War. One of 16 children, he and four of his brothers all fought at the Battle of Waterloo.

MARKET DRAYTON, HODNET HALL 1899 44454
Home to the Heber-Percy family, Hodnet Hall was only built in the 19th century, despite its Elizabethan style. Henry Heber, rector in the village of Hodnet for a time, wrote the hymn 'Holy, Holy, Holy, Lord God Almighty'.

STYCHE HALL, BIRTHPLACE OF LORD CLIVE 1898 42231

STYCHE HALL
Birthplace of Lord Clive 1898
Robert Clive, Clive of India, was born in 1725. At the age of 18 he joined the East India Company as a clerk, but soon transferred to their army fighting against the French for control of the sub-continent. His most famous victory was at the Battle of Plassey where, with 3,000 men, he defeated an army of 68,000.

MARKET DRAYTON
From The South 1898
Local histories describe Robert Clive as a young tearaway, and stories of him abound. He ran a protection racket, for example, and with his young gang of hooligans dammed a stream through the town so that it flooded the shop of a butcher who would not pay him protection money - or so the story goes!

MARKET DRAYTON, FROM THE SOUTH 1898 42198

MARKET DRAYTON, FROM THE SOUTH 1898 42199a

Market Drayton stands on a hill-top site overlooking the River Tern, which flows in the foreground of this photograph, and the settlement probably originated in prehistoric times. In medieval times it was a market town owned by Combermere Abbey, a Cistercian abbey on the Cheshire border.

MARKET DRAYTON, BUTTER CROSS 1911 63339

Northern Shropshire is famous for its cheeses and dairy products, hence the market (or Buttercross) in the picture, which was built in 1824. The town once had a court of 'pied poudre'; here litigants could settle their differences immediately they reached market - in other words, while they still had dusty (or powdered) feet.

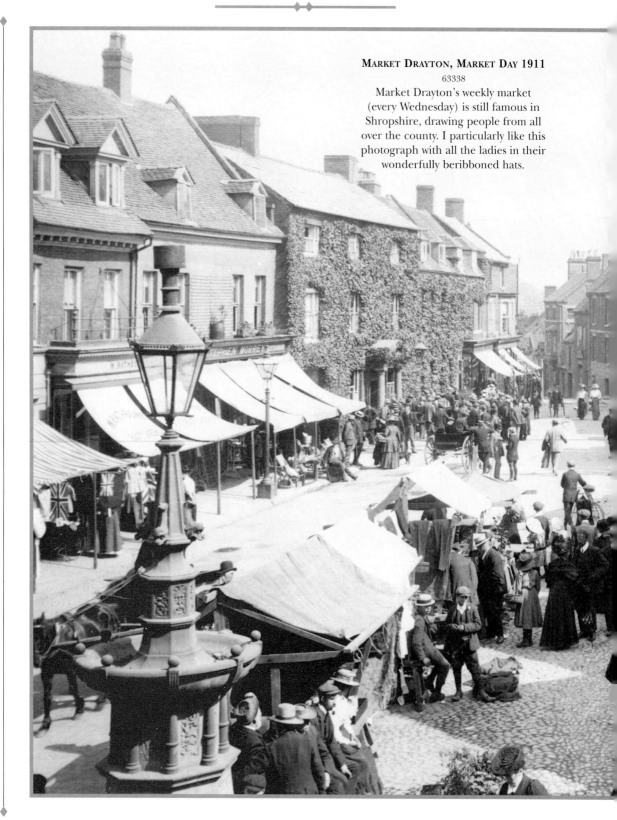

MARKET DRAYTON, MARKET DAY 1911
63338
Market Drayton's weekly market (every Wednesday) is still famous in Shropshire, drawing people from all over the county. I particularly like this photograph with all the ladies in their wonderfully beribboned hats.

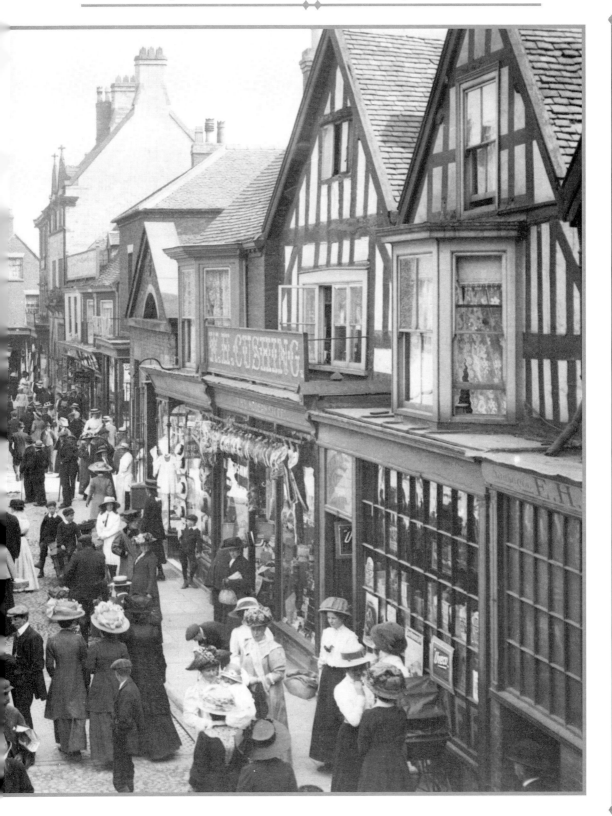

MARKET DRAYTON, HIGH STREET 1903 50717
Returning from India with a taste for spicy food, Robert Clive is thought to have introduced ginger-bread, a product for which the town is now famous. To eat ginger-bread correctly it should be cut into slices and dunked in a glass of port. Perhaps ginger-bread was sold by W Cushing, Provisions and Groceries.

MARKET DRAYTON, SHROPSHIRE STREET 1898 42202
It was in Shropshire Street that Roland Lateward lived at the end of the 1700s. He is reputed to have been the first gingerbread baker in the town. Even today, gingerbread is still produced here.

MARKET DRAYTON, SHROPSHIRE STREET 1899 44432
Posters everywhere are advertising Herbert Bowdler's summer sale for '14 days only'. How unlike today, when sales sometimes seem to go on for months. Today, this building is known as the Tudor House and is a hotel.

MARKET DRAYTON, SHROPSHIRE STREET, OLD HOUSE 1898 42203
Shropshire towns have long had a reputation for their displays of hanging baskets and window boxes, a fashion that the rest of the country seems only recently to have followed. Notice the rusticated window boxes on the cottage here.

MARKET DRAYTON, THE CORBET ARMS HOTEL 1911 63336

MARKET DRAYTON
The Corbet Arms Hotel 1911
The Corbet Arms Hotel is named for an important Shropshire family that came to England with William the Conqueror. Their name comes from the French word for a raven, and so throughout the county there are many examples of hotels and inns called either the Corbet Arms or the Raven.

◆

MARKET DRAYTON
High Street 1923
Twelve years pass by, and very little seems to change. The hotel is said to be haunted by a young girl who was abandoned by her lover and so committed suicide here. When good-looking bachelors occupy the room in which she died she occasionally pinches their bottoms!

MARKET DRAYTON, HIGH STREET 1923 73791

MARKET DRAYTON, ADDERLEY HALL 1898 42206

Adderley was the scene of a feud between two local families, the Corbets and the Needhams, over fox-hunting. The Needhams thought it was a bloodthirsty sport and refused to allow the Corbets to hunt over their lands; arguments between the two families continued for years.

PELWELL HALL, THE GARAGE 1911 63377

Pelwell Hall was built in the 1820s by the architect Sir John Soane. In recent years, having been abandoned, vandalised and finally set on fire, it has become a ruin; it is currently being restored. The stable block in the picture has remained in use, however.

MARKET DRAYTON, TYRLEY LOCKS 1911 63346

MARKET DRAYTON
Tyrley Locks 1911
Now known as the Shropshire Union Canal, this was originally the Birmingham and Liverpool Junction Canal; it was the last of Thomas Telford's canals, being completed six months after he died. Notice the little girl with her white pinny and the horse with its nosebox.

◆

MARKET DRAYTON
Norton Village 1899
Here the brickwork of the houses has been used for a very decorative effect. Notice the already well-established monkey puzzle tree. These originally came from Chile. The Victorians were very keen plant collectors, and introduced an immense range of plants to gardens around Britain.

MARKET DRAYTON, NORTON VILLAGE 1899 44460

NEWPORT, HIGH STREET AND THE CHURCH 1898 41983

St Nicholas's church stands on its own island surrounded by streets. St Nicholas was the patron saint of fishermen; much of the town's early wealth was based on its many fish ponds When the king was in the area, the town was obliged to supply his court with fresh fish.

NEWPORT, HIGH STREET 1898 41979

Originally the word 'port' meant market - so the name reminds us that this was a new market town, laid out in the early 12th century when Henry I granted the settlement a special charter. Today's buildings still follow the lines of the original burgage plots laid out all that time ago.

NEWPORT, HIGH STREET C1965 N26024

The tower of the church dates from the 14th century. Otherwise, much of the church was rebuilt in the late 1800s. Inside is a wonderful window by William Morris and Edward Burne-Jones that dates to the 1870s.

NEWPORT, HIGH STREET C1960 N26015

Today's health and safety regulations would never allow the petrol pump to be positioned in the middle of a public pavement! The building just behind the pump houses a 'circulating library' as well as the W H Smith bookshop.

NEWPORT, HIGH STREET 1898 41980
In 1665 Newport suffered a great fire, so there are few really old buildings in the town. One of the older ones is the Shakespeare Inn; Shakespeare's bust still adorns this pub today.

NEWPORT, HIGH STREET 1898 41981
Newport has a famous school founded in the 17th century. It was one of the schoolboys here, Thomas Brown, who coined the rhyme (about a master): 'I do not love thee, Dr Fell, The reason why I cannot tell, But this I know, and know full well, I do not love thee, Dr Fell'.

NEWPORT, HIGH STREET 1893 41982
Charles Dickens visited Newport,
where he heard the story of a local
recluse, Elizabeth Parker, who had
been jilted on her wedding day.
Today the house Elizabeth lived in
has been converted into flats and
is known as Havisham Court,
after Miss Havisham in
'Great Expectations'.

NEWPORT, ON THE CANAL 1898 41991

NEWPORT
On the Canal 1898

This branch line canal was built to link with Telford's last canal, the Shropshire Union canal. Horses pulling the narrowboats would have climbed up the bridge on the right and down on the left, thus changing from one side of the canal to the other at this point.

◆

NEWPORT
Canal Port c1955

Compare this with the picture above, taken over 50 years earlier. Once the canals ceased to be used for the transport of goods, it did not take long for them to become silted up and overgrown. Notice the route of the towpath going over the bridge. Much of the canal was restored in the 1970s.

NEWPORT, CANAL PORT c1955 N26002

NEWPORT
On the Canal 1898
A horse is just emerging under the bridge pulling a laden narrow-boat. Canals totally changed the transportation of goods around the country - in fact, once a string of boats started to move, it was possible for a single horse to pull up to 20 boats, each laden with up to seven tons of coal.

◆

NEWPORT
On the Canal 1898
With so many canals recently restored for leisure purposes, this is a scene that is still very familiar to fishermen, walkers and boat people all over the country.

NEWPORT, ON THE CANAL 1898 41992

NEWPORT, ON THE CANAL 1898 41990

BOSCOBEL, BOSCOBEL HOUSE 1898 41885

The story of Charles II hiding in an oak tree is true - it happened here, in what was then thickly wooded countryside. Hiding in the tree by day, he hid in a priest's hole in Boscobel House at night until the Roundheads abandoned their search and he was able to make his way to safety.

TONG, THE VILLAGE (HOME OF DICKENS' 'LITTLE HALL') 1898 41858

There is hardly anywhere in England that Charles Dickens did not visit and then use in a story. It was in Tong that he buried Little Nell in his book 'The Old Curiosity Shop', and so immediately gave rise to a thriving local tourist industry for visitors to see her grave. The grave is still there!

TONG, THE BELL INN 1902 48807

Tong gets its name from an old Anglo-Saxon word for fork: here it comes from the shape of two streams coming together to form one. Tong's church, St Bartholomew's, is particularly beautiful, and is known as the Westminster of the Midlands. It has a superb fan-vaulted ceiling.

TONG, THE CASTLE 1898 41853

Built in the late 1700s by 'Capability' Brown, who is usually better known for his gardens, this extravagant mansion was demolished in 1954. Today the M54 motorway runs right over the site.

BUILDWAS, THE ABBEY FROM THE FERRY 38115

BUILDWAS
The Abbey from the Ferry
The ruined monastery at Buildwas is the most complete of all such ruins in the county. A Cistercian monastery, it was founded in the early 1100s and sited beside the River Severn so that it could take advantage of the trading links along the river. At one time the monks even ran their own ironworks.

BUILDWAS
The Village c1955
The name Buildwas is thought to come from Old English, meaning 'a building in a swamp'. Certainly the fertile flood plain of the river is good farming land, but at this point, just before the Severn enters the Ironbridge Gorge, it is regularly subject to flooding.

BUILDWAS, THE VILLAGE C1955 B244005

IRONBRIDGE, FROM THE WEST 1896 38106

The iron bridge, for which the town is now named, was built in 1779. Although heralding a change in technology, it uses old technology in its construction - the joints are all timber carpenter's joints. The bridge was built very much as an advertisement for the area - to prove how versatile iron could be.

IRONBRIDGE, THE BRIDGE 1904 51376

The bridge was a toll bridge; it opened to the public on 1 January 1781. The toll house is the brick building on the left - a sign lists the charges, stating that because the bridge is privately owned, even soldiers on duty AND the Royal Family are obliged to pay to cross over.

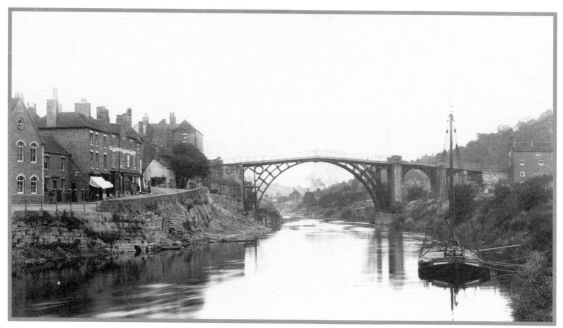

IRONBRIDGE, THE BRIDGE FROM THE RIVER 1892 30891

Notice the river boat, or trow, moored to the bank. At one time the River Severn was one of the busiest in Europe, and trade along it was dependent on these boats. The shallow draught of the trow was essential along a river like this with its sand banks and low summer water levels.

IRONBRIDGE, FROM THE ROTUNDA 1892 30892

By the time this photograph was taken Ironbridge was no longer the industrial heartland it had once been. Much of the heavy industry had already moved to the Black Country, Lancashire, south Wales etc. Yet one can still sense the pall of smoke that lies over all of the buildings in the valley.

IRONBRIDGE
From the South 1896

The iron bridge is in the foreground. Immediately opposite is a Georgian building - the Tontine Hotel. When the bridge was built, people came from all over the world to see it. So many people came, in fact, that the hotel was opened in 1783 especially to cater for them all.

◆

IRONBRIDGE
From the Opposite Hill 1896

Many people avoided paying the tolls on the bridge by rowing coracles across the river. It was here, too, that a boy named Matthew Webb learnt to swim. He was later to become the first man to swim across the English Channel in 1875. He later died trying to swim across the Niagara Falls.

IRONBRIDGE, FROM THE SOUTH 1896 38110

IRONBRIDGE, FROM THE OPPOSITE HILL 1896 38109

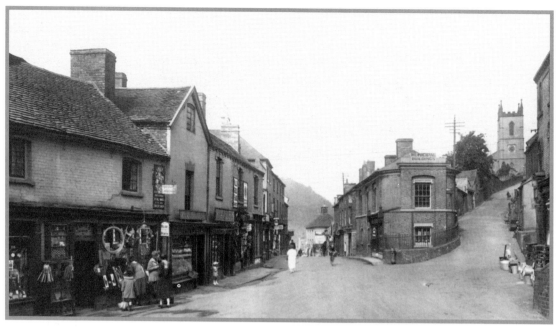

IRONBRIDGE, HIGH STREET AND CHURCH STREET 1925 76923

Today the area around Ironbridge is a World Heritage Site: many of the old workshops, factories etc are being restored or converted into museums. These include the Blist's Hill Museum (with many restored buildings), a museum of iron, a china museum, a tile-making museum, and even a restored police station.

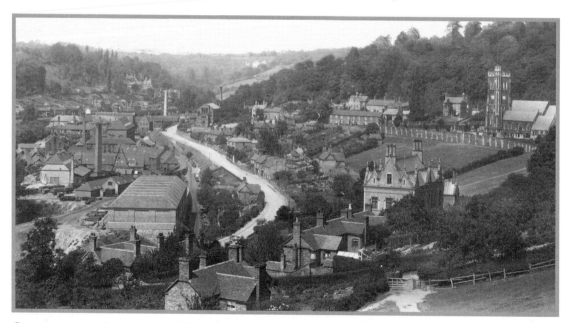

COALBROOKDALE, GENERAL VIEW 1896 38112

It was here, two miles from Ironbridge, that the industrial revolution began. Abraham Darby bought a furnace in 1706 and began experimenting with ways of smelting iron by using coke rather than charcoal In 1709 he mastered the technique and changed the world. It was his grandson, Abraham Darby III, who later built the famous bridge.

COALBROOKDALE, DALE ROAD 1896 38111
As it was never a very prosperous area, there are few early buildings of interest in and around Ironbridge and Coalbrookdale. The timber building here, Rose Cottage, is a rare survival.

WELLINGTON, CHURCH STREET 1903 51130
Wellington has always been a prosperous small market town. It sits beside the old Roman road of Watling Street, and later benefited from toll-roads and railways. After the iron bridge was built, its trading area grew: it now attracted people south of the river, who previously would have used the market at Much Wenlock.

WELLINGTON, MARKET SQUARE 1903 51132
Notice all the evidence of day-to-day trade,
especially the delivery boys with parcels or
newspapers. Also, by this time we often see names
that we now know very well - on the wall at the
end of the street is a sign for Boots, described
here as 'Cash Chemists - Largest in the World'.

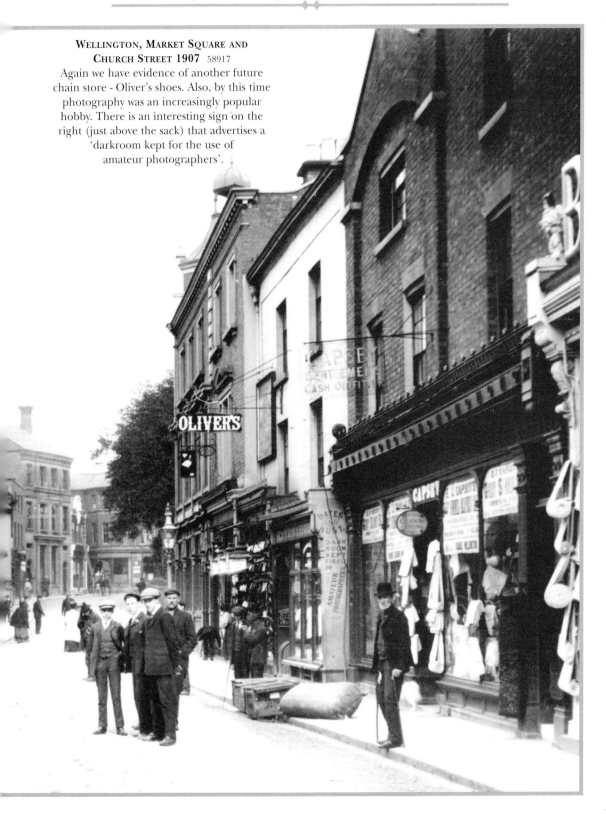

WELLINGTON, MARKET SQUARE AND CHURCH STREET 1907 58917
Again we have evidence of another future chain store - Oliver's shoes. Also, by this time photography was an increasingly popular hobby. There is an interesting sign on the right (just above the sack) that advertises a 'darkroom kept for the use of amateur photographers'.

WELLINGTON, CHURCH STREET 1907 58918
Hesba Stretton is a little-known writer who was born in Wellington. Her real name was Sarah Smith, and she wrote novels with a strong religious theme. One novel, 'Jessica's First Prayer', was published in 1866 and sold one and a half million copies. She was also a founder member of what is now the NSPCC.

WELLINGTON, NEW STREET 1907 58919

This street is now pedestrianised. Judging from the photograph, perhaps in a sense it always has been. One gets the distinct impression that all the children here have been carefully posed by the photographer. It is interesting to note how smartly dressed they all are, as they would not have been very well-off.

WELLINGTON, THE FOREST GLEN 1895 35969

The Refreshment Pavilion (see the writing on the roof) served walkers visiting the Wrekin, one of the finest viewpoints in Shropshire. It is said that two giants were digging in the area to form the valley of the River Severn, and the Wrekin was formed from all the spoil they dug out.

THE WREKIN, THE NEEDLE'S EYE 1895 35977
The same two giants later had an argument, and one of them threw his spade at the other. The spade missed, but struck the hill instead, causing the gash now known as the Needle's Eye. Walking clothes seem to have changed considerably in the last one hundred years.

DAWLEY, HIGH STREET c1955 D169009

Dawley and Wellington were rivals to control Shropshire's new town. People here wanted to call it Dawley New Town. Those in Wellington (not to mention all the smaller towns and villages) refused point blank. Finally a compromise was reached - it was named Telford after the Scottish engineer, Thomas Telford, who did so much work locally.

OAKENGATES, THE CLOCK AND POST OFFICE 1900 46150

Like Dawley, Oakengates sits on old coal mines and iron works, which have all now closed down. The workers in these industries were often very rough: the area was known for its drunken orgies, riotous wakes and blood sports - the last bull-baiting in the county took place here in 1833.

OAKENGATES, MARKET STREET 1899 44139

Oakengates' most famous personality was the son of a local coal-miner. Sir Gordon Richards (born in 1904) won his first race at Leicester in 1921; by the time he retired, he had ridden 4,870 winners - truly a Champion Jockey, the name of a pub in nearby Donnington!

OAKENGATES, MARKET STREET c1955 O1020

Here we see the same street some fifty years later. Only the traffic and styles of dress seem to have changed. The bridge at the far end of the road is for the railway line - the Great Western Railway or, as railway enthusiasts would usually describe it, 'God's Wonderful Railway'.

OAKENGATES, MARKET STREET C1955 O1010

This is the same street again but looking in the opposite direction. This was the period that saw the beginning of the end for the town - in 1959 the last steel works closed, followed in 1987 by the last iron works.

OAKENGATES, OXFORD STREET C1955 O1023

Today every street in the country seems to have lines, arrows and commands painted all over it. We forget what a recent introduction this is; a comparison of this photograph with the next one (of the same street but from the other direction) shows that by the early 1960s the 'Keep Clear' signs had arrived.

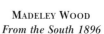

OAKENGATES
Oxford Street c1965
Note how within ten years the style of all the cars has also totally changed.

◆

MADELEY WOOD
From the South 1896
Such a pretty name, such an ugly town. Linking Madeley and Ironbridge, this area grew rapidly in the 18th century as local industry expanded. The most famous iron furnace here was the 'Bedlam Furnace': with its flames and smoke, and noise and grime, it must have seemed like the very gates of Hell.

OAKENGATES, OXFORD STREET c1965 O1041

MADELEY WOOD, FROM THE SOUTH 1896 38120a

MADELEY, OLD COURT HOUSE 1896 38118

The Court House gets its name because it was once, in the 16th century, the home of a leading lawyer and speaker in the House of Commons. The most famous resident, however, was Abraham Darby, who lived here for a time after he arrived in the area. The building has recently been restored and is now a hotel.

BROSELEY, HIGH STREET 1904 51385

The blurred images of the children in the foreground remind us of the long exposure times photographers needed in those days. Coal was exported downriver from here - in 1756, 87 boats were registered in Broseley to transport coal. Local businessmen were also keen investors in the iron bridge, which opened markets to the north.

HADLEY, THE VILLAGE 1901 47324

The pub is called the Old Bush Inn. This is an old name for a pub; it dates back to times when the brewer would hang a bit of a bush over the front door to advertise that a new brew was ready. This gave rise to the saying 'a good ale needs no bush'.

HADLEY, THE CASTLE CAR WORKS 1902 48814

The factory whistle has just blown, and all the workers are on their way home. The two gates pictured show the 'workmen's entrances' as opposed to the main entrance. During World War II the factory produced spitfire parts, mines and bombs.

HADLEY
The Castle Car Works 1902
The canal by the side of the factory was built to serve all the local industries and factories. However, by 1902 all the business was going by rail, and already the canal appears to be falling into disrepair.

◆

LILLESHALL
The Village 1898
At the time of the Industrial Revolution the people of Lilleshall, until then mainly a farming community, began mining limestone to supply the iron-smelting industry at Coalbrookdale. The mines were flooded at the end of the 19th century and the workings ceased.

HADLEY, THE CASTLE CAR WORKS 1902 48812

LILLESHALL, THE VILLAGE 1898 41851

ALBRIGHTON, THE VILLAGE 1898 41878
Albrighton is a very pretty name for a village. Actually there are two Albrightons in Shropshire - the meanings for which originally differed. One was Aethelbeorht's farmstead (this village), and the other was Eadbeorht's farmstead. Over the centuries the names evolved to become the same.

ALBRIGHTON, THE VILLAGE 1898 41877
Today Albrighton is known to most people because of its proximity to the RAF base at nearby Cosford. The airbase is also home to one of the largest air museums in the country, with both military and civilian aircraft on display.

ALBRIGHTON
The Village 1899

A scene that could have been copied in any town or village in the country in 1899. Notice particularly the pot plants on the porch of the nearby house, and also the horse droppings in the roadway.

Halfway between Telford and Wolverhampton, Albrighton now serves as a dormitory for both the other towns.

◆

SHIFNAL
Market Place 1898

Shifnal is thought to have been the model for P G Wodehouse's 'Market Blandings'. The road here has since been widened with the demolition of the butcher's shop - can you see the legs of meat hanging outside the window of Mason's?

ALBRIGHTON, THE VILLAGE 1899 44171

SHIFNAL, MARKET PLACE 1898 41818

SHIFNAL, MARKET PLACE 1899 44150
Sometimes a lot of change can take place in a very short time. Notice how the butcher's shop has obviously just been repainted. Mr Mason (?) still stands by the door, meat still hangs outside the window, but the sign has not yet been replaced.

BRIDGNORTH, THE BRIDGE 1898 42624
Bridgnorth has always been divided in two: High Town on a defensive position on the hill, and Low Town for traders by the river. The two are linked by numerous steep, narrow lanes and by a cliff railway, a sign to which has been painted on the top of the building on the left.

BRIDGNORTH, HIGH STREET 1896 38126
It is remarkable that the Town Hall still almost totally blocks the town's High Street. It was built in 1652. Francis Moore, whose 'Old Moore's Almanac' is still published every year, was born in Bridgnorth. His first almanac was called Vox Stellarum (Voice of the Stars) and was published over 300 years ago.

BRIDGNORTH, THE LIFT 1898 42631
The lift railway was still very new when this photograph was taken - it was built in 1891. Rising 111 feet high up the cliff, it is 201 feet long. The town is also a centre for another type of railway - the restored Severn Valley Railway with its steam engines.

BRIDGNORTH, NORTHGATE 1896 38127

Bridgnorth, as a fortified hill-top site, dates from Saxon times. Visiting the town at the beginning of the Civil War, Charles I described the view from the castle ramparts as 'the finest in my kingdom'. Mind you, he was looking for finance from the locals, and so he may have been laying on the charm.

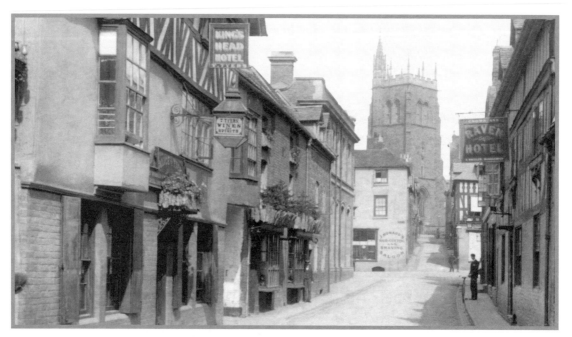

BRIDGNORTH, WHITBURN STREET 1898 42630

St Leonard's church was at the heart of the civilian community at one end of the hill, with the castle at the other end and the High Street with its market linking the two. Today the church, now redundant, is the venue for an annual Haydn festival.

BRIDGNORTH
The Hermitage 1896

The town and castle sit on a cliff of very soft sandstone. Over the years dwellings were carved out within the stone and, as can be seen from the curtains in the windows, these were occupied into the 20th century.

OLDBURY
Canal Boats c1930

In medieval times, Bridgnorth was the second most important town in Shropshire owing to its position on the junction of two trade routes - river traffic to north and south, road traffic to east and west. At Oldbury, now a suburb, river boats would collect, waiting for their turn to dock in Bridgnorth and unload.

BRIDGNORTH, THE HERMITAGE 1896 38136

OLDBURY, CANAL BOATS c1930 O128501

LUDLOW, THE CASTLE FROM QUARRY 1896 38149

With its castle and town established by the Normans at the end of the 11th century, Ludlow was later to become a most important military base controlling the Welsh Marches (or borders). In fact, by Tudor times the entire Welsh principality was being governed from Ludlow.

LUDLOW, THE CASTLE FROM THE RIVER 1923 73772

It was here that the newly married Prince Arthur brought his bride, Katherine of Aragon. Within six months, Arthur had died and Katherine was betrothed to his younger brother Henry, later Henry VIII. Following their divorce, Katherine and Henry's daughter, Princess Mary, lived here for a time. We now know her as Bloody Mary.

LUDLOW, THE CASTLE ENTRANCE 1910 62479
The castle has been owned by the Earls of Powys since the early 1800s, and they have always opened it to the public. The sign on the door announces that admission will cost 6d (or 2½ new pence!).

LUDLOW, THE CASTLE c1960 L111103
Ludlow Castle has been associated with many monarchs. It was the principal seat of the Mortimer family, one of whom became Edward IV. His two sons, Edward and Richard, lived here before being taken to The Tower of London, never to be seen again - they were the two young 'Princes in the Tower'.

LUDLOW, THE CASTLE AND THE ROUND CHAPEL 1892 30817
The round building is all that survives of the former castle chapel. It is actually the nave of the chapel; the chancel (which would have been on the right) was long since demolished. Round chapels are extremely rare: this one was built by the Knights Templar, a crusading order, in the 12th century.

LUDLOW
Dinham Bridge and Castle Hill 1892
The building in the trees to the right of the picture is Dinham Hall. It was used in the early 1800s to imprison Lucien Bonaparte, Napoleon's brother. He lived here with an entourage which included his wife, seven children and 23 servants.

LUDLOW
Ludford Bridge 1892
The first bridge on this site was built in the 12th century; this one dates from the 15th century, but probably incorporates part of the earlier structure.

LUDLOW, DINHAM BRIDGE AND CASTLE HILL 1892 30821

LUDLOW, LUDFORD BRIDGE 1892 30823

LUDLOW, LOWER BROAD STREET 1892 30825

In 1233 the town of Ludlow was given permission to build town walls. Originally there were seven town gates (four main and three postern). This is the southern gate, and the only one surviving today. It is (most inappropriately, I think) known as the Broadgate.

LUDLOW, BROADGATE, c1960 L111119

The little building to the right of the gate has now become an inn - the Wheatsheaf. Tradition states that it is linked to the castle by a tunnel. This is unlikely. The story has probably arisen because the inn sits over the former ditch that would have surrounded the town walls immediately behind it.

LUDLOW, THE MARKET HALL 1892 30828
This building is described by Nikolaus Pevsner as 'Ludlow's bad luck . . . there is nothing that could be said in (its) favour'. The market hall was built in 1888 at a cost of £6,000; it lasted less than 100 years, being demolished in 1986.

LUDLOW, THE OLD BELL INN, LUDFORD 1892 30834
Ludford was the name given to the settlement beside the bridge at the southern entrance to Ludlow. It is thought that the 'Lud' element in each placename refers to a man of that name. This was the ford by Lud's burial mound (or 'low') which sat on the top of the hill under the present church.

LUDLOW, THE FEATHERS HOTEL 1892 30829
It is generally agreed by those outside the profession that lawyers charge too much. Here is the evidence. This house was built by a lawyer in the early 1600s. By the end of that century it had become an inn with stabling for 100 horses. The carved balcony above the doorway is a 19th century addition.

LUDLOW, THE BULL RING AND THE FEATHERS HOTEL 1936 87396

LUDLOW
The Bull Ring and the Feathers Hotel 1936
'. . . come you home of Monday When Ludlow market hums . . .' Once this area was the entrance to Ludlow's market, with traders paying tolls at the nearby Tolsey (or toll booth). The ashes of A E Housman, who wrote the above lines in 'A Shropshire Lad', are buried here in St Lawrence's churchyard.

◆

LUDLOW
Corve Street 1910
Corve Street is the main road leading north to Shrewsbury. Notice the way that the road suddenly becomes that little bit wider. The photographer was standing on the position of the old town wall/boundary. Beyond the wall there would have been more room to spread out, and so immediately the road becomes much wider.

LUDLOW, CORVE STREET 1910 62477

LUDLOW, THE LECTURER'S HOUSE 1923 73778

In medieval times the Palmer's Guild was the most powerful guild in Ludlow, but it was dissolved in the 16th century. Its assets were transferred to the town by charter in 1551. The appointment of a public preacher was paid from these funds, and this house was built in 1611 to house the town's Preacher.

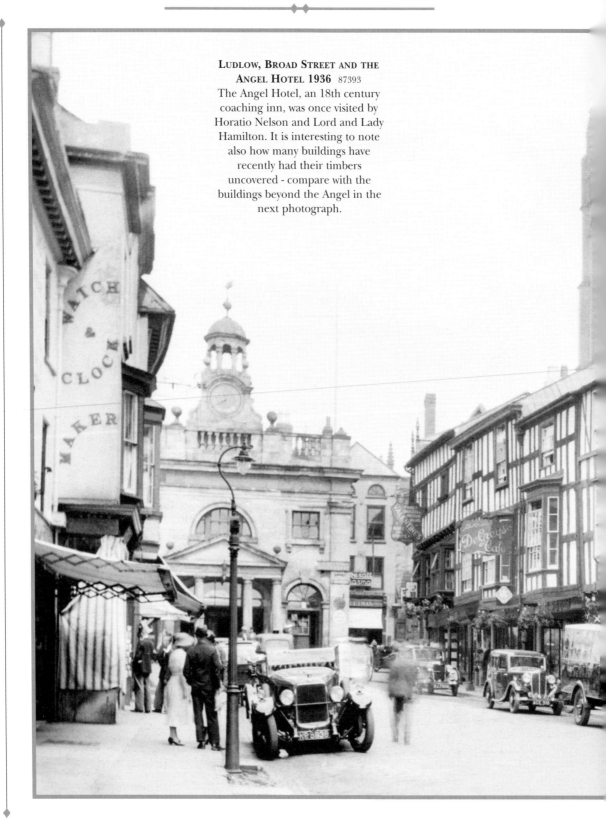

**LUDLOW, BROAD STREET AND THE
ANGEL HOTEL 1936** 87393
The Angel Hotel, an 18th century
coaching inn, was once visited by
Horatio Nelson and Lord and Lady
Hamilton. It is interesting to note
also how many buildings have
recently had their timbers
uncovered - compare with the
buildings beyond the Angel in the
next photograph.

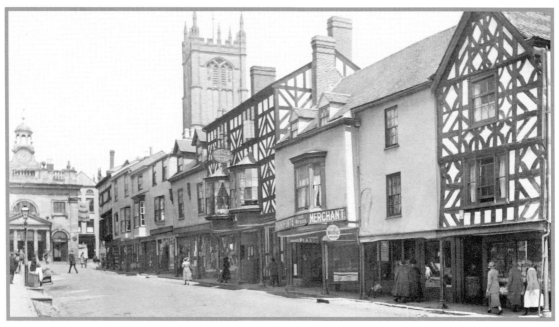

LUDLOW, BROAD STREET 1923 73782

Broad Street was described by Nikolaus Pevsner as 'one of the most memorable streets in England'. It is a wonderful mix of architectural styles, with 15th-century buildings at the top and elegant Georgian further downhill, all overlooked by the tower of St Lawrence's church, the largest parish church in Shropshire.

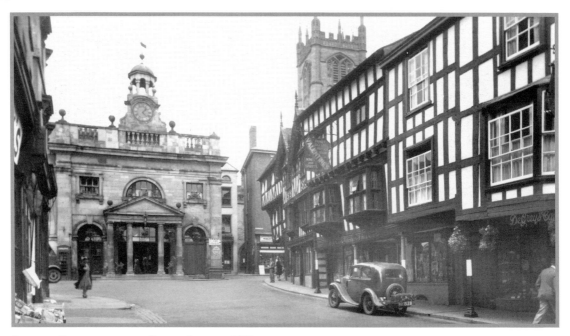

LUDLOW, BUTTERCROSS AND BROAD STREET c1955 L111035

The Buttercross was built in 1744 at a cost of £1,000. The ground floor served as a butter market, hence the name. Upstairs was the Blue Coat Charity School (the name came from the uniforms given to the boys to wear). The cupola on top is thought to have come from St Leonard's chapel in nearby Corve Street.

LUDLOW, KING STREET 1936 87395

The sign on the stone building ahead reads 'Caution Leominster'. It is a sign that modern coach and truck drivers would still need to heed. They regularly bang into the overhanging timber building on the left; its timbers have been dated to 1403/04.

BROMFIELD, THE CHURCH FROM THE BRIDGE 1904 51654
Henry Hill Hickman was born here and is buried in the church. By the age of 21 he was a member of the Royal College of Surgeons. He was a pioneer in the science of anaesthetics, but although he tried to publicise his work, no-one then was interested. He died in 1830 aged only 30.

BROMFIELD, THE CHURCH 1924 76178

The chancel ceiling of St Mary's church in Bromfield was painted in 1672. It is absolutely hideous, and yet somehow one cannot help rather liking it. It has been described, very aptly, as being the 'best example of the worst style of ecclesiastical art'.

STOKESAY
The Castle c1960

Stokesay Castle has to be one of the most romantic medieval sites in the country. It has a bad defensive position for a castle, though, so that when it was attacked during the Civil War the defenders wisely abandoned it and took refuge in the church instead. As a result it fortunately survived the war.

◆

STOKESAY
The Castle 1910

In the early 1600s Stokesay was owned by Lord Craven. He fell in love with Elizabeth of Bohemia (sister to Charles I); rumour has it that they secretly married after the death of her husband, Frederick of Hanover. Lord Craven refurbished Stokesay for Elizabeth; it is sad to think that she never even came here.

STOKESAY, THE CASTLE c1960 S202024

STOKESAY, THE CASTLE 1910 62491

STOKESAY, THE CASTLE FROM THE CHURCHYARD c1864 2239

Much of the castle was built at the end of the 1200s by Lawrence de Ludlow, a wealthy wool merchant. At this time England's wealth lay in its wool. In fact, by the end of the 13th century half of England's entire revenue came from wool.

STOKESAY, THE CASTLE GATEHOUSE 1924 76219

Following the castle's capture in the Civil War, the original stone gatehouse was destroyed. This timber gatehouse therefore dates from the late 1600s. It is very ornately carved - notice, for example, the carved head on the corner post to the left.

CRAVEN ARMS, MARKET STREET c1960 C539014

Craven Arms - a town named for its pub! Actually, it is named for the Earls of Craven, who also owned nearby Stokesay Castle. This town sits on an old meeting point - Roman roads, 18th-century toll roads and railways all crossed through here.

CLEE HILL c1960 C505039

In his 'A Shropshire Lad', the poet A E Housman opens with the words: 'From Clee to heaven the beacon burns, The shires have seen it plain . . .' The high, windswept Clee Hills would have been an excellent place to light a beacon celebrating Victoria's jubilee, the occasion described in this poem.

CLEOBURY MORTIMER, CHURCH STREET c1955 C506030
Pronounced 'clibbery', Cleobury Mortimer is famous for the crooked spire of its church. The town also claims to be the birthplace of William Langland, a poet living at the same time as Chaucer, whose masterpiece is the work 'The Vision of Piers the Plowman'.

CHIRBURY, THE VILLAGE c1955 C504011
Chirbury was the home of Lord Herbert, an Elizabethan philosopher, diplomat and keen historian. He collected a large library of chained books (the books were chained to their shelves so that they could not be taken away) which he bequeathed to the villagers. The books are now kept in the main library in Shrewsbury.

CLUN, THE BRIDGE C1960 C507050
Clun means 'church', from the Celtic 'clon' and Welsh 'llan'. The old Saxon church with its settlement were to the right of the river, the Norman castle and market to the left. This medieval saddleback bridge, which dates from around 1450, links the two parts of the town.

Index

Frith Book Co Titles

www.francisfrith.co.uk

The Frith Book Company publishes over 100 new titles each year. A selection of those currently available are listed below. For latest catalogue please contact Frith Book Co.

Town Books 96pp, 100 photos. County and Themed Books 128pp, 150 photos (unless specified). All titles hardback laminated case and jacket except those indicated pb (paperback)

Title	Code	Price
Ancient Monuments & Stone Circles	143-4	£17.99
Aylesbury (pb)	227-9	£9.99
Bakewell	113-2	£12.99
Barnstaple (pb)	300-3	£9.99
Bath (pb)	419-0	£9.99
Bedford (pb)	205-8	£9.99
Berkshire (pb)	191-4	£9.99
Berkshire Churches	170-1	£17.99
Bognor Regis (pb)	431-x	£9.99
Bournemouth	067-5	£12.99
Bradford (pb)	204-x	£9.99
Brighton & Hove (pb)	192-2	£8.99
Bristol (pb)	264-3	£9.99
British Life A Century Ago (pb)	213-9	£9.99
Buckinghamshire (pb)	200-7	£9.99
Camberley (pb)	222-8	£9.99
Cambridge (pb)	422-0	£9.99
Cambridgeshire (pb)	420-4	£9.99
Canals & Waterways (pb)	291-0	£9.99
Cardiff (pb)	093-4	£9.99
Carmarthenshire	216-3	£14.99
Cheltenham (pb)	095-0	£9.99
Cheshire (pb)	271-6	£9.99
Chester	090-x	£12.99
Chesterfield	071-3	£12.99
Chichester (pb)	228-7	£9.99
Colchester (pb)	188-4	£8.99
Cornish Coast	163-9	£14.99
Cornwall (pb)	229-5	£9.99
Cornwall Living Memories	248-1	£14.99
Cotswolds (pb)	230-9	£9.99
Cotswolds Living Memories	255-4	£14.99
County Durham	123-x	£14.99
Cumbria	101-9	£14.99
Dartmoor	145-0	£14.99
Derbyshire (pb)	196-5	£9.99
Devon (pb)	297-x	£9.99
Dorset (pb)	269-4	£9.99
Dorset Churches	172-8	£17.99
Dorset Coast (pb)	299-6	£9.99
Dorset Living Memories	210-4	£14.99
Down the Severn	118-3	£14.99
Down the Thames (pb)	278-3	£9.99
Dublin (pb)	231-7	£9.99
East Anglia (pb)	265-1	£9.99
East London	080-2	£14.99
East Sussex	130-2	£14.99
Eastbourne	061-6	£12.99
Edinburgh (pb)	193-0	£8.99
English Castles (pb)	434-4	£9.99
English Country Houses	161-2	£17.99
Exeter	126-4	£12.99
Exmoor	132-9	£14.99
Falmouth	066-7	£12.99
Folkestone (pb)	124-8	£9.99
Glasgow (pb)	190-6	£9.99
Gloucestershire	102-7	£14.99
Greater Manchester (pb)	266-x	£9.99
Harrogate	423-9	£12.99
Hampshire Churches (pb)	131-0	£9.99
Hastings & Bexhill (pb)	131-0	£9.99
Heart of Lancashire (pb)	197-3	£9.99
Helston	214-7	£9.99
Hereford (pb)	175-2	£9.99
Herefordshire	174-4	£14.99
Humberside	215-5	£14.99
Hythe, Romney Marsh & Ashford	256-2	£9.99
Ipswich (pb)	424-7	£9.99
Ireland (pb)	181-7	£9.99
Isles of Scilly	136-1	£14.99
Isle of Wight Living Memories	304-6	£14.99
Kent (pb)	189-2	£9.99
Kent Living Memories	125-6	£14.99
Lake District (pb)	275-9	£9.99
Lancaster, Morecambe & Heysham (pb)	233-3	£9.99
Leeds (pb)	202-3	£9.99
Leicester	073-x	£12.99
Leicestershire (pb)	185-x	£9.99
Lincolnshire (pb)	433-6	£9.99
Liverpool & Merseyside (pb)	234-1	£9.99
London (pb)	183-3	£9.99
Ludlow (pb)	176-0	£9.99
Luton (pb)	235-x	£9.99
Manchester (pb)	198-1	£9.99
New Forest	128-0	£14.99
Newport, Wales (pb)	258-9	£9.99
Newquay (pb)	421-2	£9.99
Norfolk (pb)	195-7	£9.99
Norfolk Living Memories	217-1	£14.99
Northamptonshire	150-7	£14.99
Northumberland Tyne & Wear (pb)	281-3	£9.99
North Devon Coast	146-9	£14.99
North Devon Living Memories	261-9	£14.99
North Wales (pb)	298-8	£9.99
North Yorkshire (pb)	236-8	£9.99
Norwich (pb)	194-9	£8.99
Nottingham (pb)	324-0	£9.99
Nottinghamshire (pb)	187-6	£9.99
Peak District (pb)	280-5	£9.99
Penzance	069-1	£12.99
Peterborough (pb)	219-8	£9.99
Piers	237-6	£17.99
Plymouth	119-1	£12.99
Poole & Sandbanks	251-1	£9.99
Preston (pb)	212-0	£9.99
Reading (pb)	238-4	£9.99
Salisbury (pb)	239-2	£9.99
St Ives	068-3	£12.99
Scotland (pb)	182-5	£9.99
Scottish Castles (pb)	323-2	£9.99
Sheffield, South Yorks (pb)	267-8	£9.99
Shrewsbury (pb)	325-9	£9.99
Somerset	153-1	£14.99
South Hams	220-1	£14.99
Southampton (pb)	427-1	£9.99
Southport (pb)	425-5	£9.99
South Devon Coast	107-8	£14.99
South Devon Living Memories	168-x	£14.99
Stratford upon Avon	098-5	£12.99
Suffolk (pb)	221-x	£9.99
Suffolk Coast	259-7	£14.99
Surrey (pb)	240-6	£9.99
Sussex (pb)	184-1	£9.99
Swansea (pb)	167-1	£9.99
Tees Valley & Cleveland	211-2	£14.99
Thanet (pb)	116-7	£9.99
Tiverton (pb)	178-7	£9.99
Torbay	063-2	£12.99
Truro	147-7	£12.99
Vic & Ed Cornwall	252-x	£14.99
Victorian & Edwardian Devon	253-8	£14.99
Victorian & Edwardian Kent	149-3	£14.99
Vic & Ed Maritime Album	144-2	£17.99
Victorian and Edwardian Sussex	157-4	£14.99
Victorian & Edwardian Yorkshire	154-x	£14.99
Victorian Seaside	159-0	£17.99
Villages of Devon (pb)	293-7	£9.99
Warwickshire (pb)	203-1	£9.99
Welsh Castles (pb)	322-4	£9.99
West Midlands (pb)	289-9	£9.99
West Sussex	148-5	£14.99
West Yorkshire (pb)	201-5	£9.99
Weymouth (pb)	209-0	£9.99
Wiltshire (pb)	277-5	£9.99
Wiltshire Churches (pb)	171-x	£9.99
Wiltshire Living Memories	245-7	£14.99
Winchester (pb)	428-x	£9.99
Windmills & Watermills	242-2	£17.99
Worcestershire	152-3	£14.99
York (pb)	199-x	£9.99
Yorkshire (pb)	186-8	£9.99
Yorkshire Living Memories	166-3	£14.99

Available from your local bookshop or from the publisher

FRITH PRODUCTS & SERVICES

Francis Frith would doubtless be pleased to know that the pioneering publishing venture he started in 1860 still continues today. A hundred and forty years later, The Francis Frith Collection continues in the same innovative tradition and is now one of the foremost publishers of vintage photographs in the world. Some of the current activities include:

Interior Decoration

Today Frith's photographs can be seen framed and as giant wall murals in thousands of pubs, restaurants, hotels, banks, retail stores and other public buildings throughout the country. In every case they enhance the unique local atmosphere of the places they depict and provide reminders of gentler days in an increasingly busy and frenetic world.

Product Promotions

Frith products are used by many major companies to promote the sales of their own products or to reinforce their own history and heritage. Frith promotions have been used by Hovis bread, Courage beers, Scots Porage Oats, Colman's mustard, Cadbury's foods, Mellow Birds coffee, Dunhill pipe tobacco, Guinness, and Bulmer's Cider.

Genealogy and Family History

As the interest in family history and roots grows world-wide, more and more people are turning to Frith's photographs of Great Britain for images of the towns, villages and streets where their ancestors lived; and, of course, photographs of the churches and chapels where their ancestors were christened, married and buried are an essential part of every genealogy tree and family album.

Frith Products

All Frith photographs are available Framed or just as Mounted Prints and Posters (size 23 x 16 inches). These may be ordered from the address below. From time to time other products - Address Books, Calendars, Table Mats, etc - are available.

The Internet

Already twenty thousand Frith photographs can be viewed and purchased on the internet through the Frith websites and a myriad of partner sites.

For more detailed information on Frith companies and products, look at these sites:

www.francisfrith.co.uk
www.francisfrith.com
(for North American visitors)

See the complete list of Frith Books at:

www.francisfrith.co.uk

This web site is regularly updated with the latest list of publications from the Frith Book Company. If you wish to buy books relating to another part of the country that your local bookshop does not stock, you may purchase on-line.

For further information, trade, or author enquiries please contact us at the address below:
The Francis Frith Collection, Frith's Barn, Teffont, Salisbury, Wiltshire, England SP3 5QP.
Tel: +44 (0)1722 716 376 Fax: +44 (0)1722 716 881 Email: sales@francisfrith.co.uk

See Frith books on the internet www.francisfrith.co.uk

TO RECEIVE YOUR FREE MOUNTED PRINT

Mounted Print
Overall size 14 x 11 inches

Cut out this Voucher and return it with your remittance for £1.95 to cover postage and handling, to UK addresses. For overseas addresses please include £4.00 post and handling. Choose any photograph included in this book. Your SEPIA print will be A4 in size, and mounted in a cream mount with burgundy rule line, overall size 14 x 11 inches.

Order additional Mounted Prints at HALF PRICE (only £7.49 each*)

If there are further pictures you would like to order, possibly as gifts for friends and family, purchase them at half price (no additional postage and handling required).

Have your Mounted Prints framed*

For an additional £14.95 per print you can have your chosen Mounted Print framed in an elegant polished wood and gilt moulding, overall size 16 x 13 inches (no additional postage and handling required).

> *** IMPORTANT!**
> These special prices are only available if ordered using the original voucher on this page (no copies permitted) and at the same time as your free Mounted Print, for delivery to the same address

Frith Collectors' Guild

From time to time we publish a magazine of news and stories about Frith photographs and further special offers of Frith products. If you would like 12 months FREE membership, please return this form.

Send completed forms to:
The Francis Frith Collection, Frith's Barn, Teffont, Salisbury, Wiltshire SP3 5QP

Voucher for **FREE** and Reduced Price Frith Prints

Picture no.	Page number	Qty	Mounted @ £7.49	Framed + £14.95	Total Cost
		1	**Free of charge***	£	£
			£7.49	£	£
			£7.49	£	£
			£7.49	£	£
			£7.49	£	£
			£7.49	£	£

Please allow 28 days for delivery	*** Post & handling**	**£1.95**
Book Title	**Total Order Cost**	**£**

Please do not photocopy this voucher. Only the original is valid, so please cut it out and return it to us.

I enclose a cheque / postal order for £ . . . .
made payable to 'The Francis Frith Collection'
OR please debit my Mastercard / Visa / Switch / Amex card
(credit cards please on all overseas orders)

Number . . . .

Issue No(Switch only) . . . . .Valid from (Amex/Switch) . . . .

Expires . . . . Signature . . . .

Name Mr/Mrs/Ms . . . .

Address . . . .

. . . .

. . . . Postcode . . . .

Daytime Tel No . . . .   Valid to 31/12/02

The Francis Frith Collectors' Guild

Please enrol me as a member for 12 months free of charge.

Name Mr/Mrs/Ms . . . .

Address . . . .

. . . .

. . . .

. . . . Postcode . . . .

Would you like to find out more about Francis Frith?

We have recently recruited some entertaining speakers who are happy to visit local groups, clubs and societies to give an illustrated talk documenting Frith's travels and photographs. If you are a member of such a group and are interested in hosting a presentation, we would love to hear from you.

Our speakers bring with them a small selection of our local town and county books, together with sample prints. They are happy to take orders. A small proportion of the order value is donated to the group who have hosted the presentation. The talks are therefore an excellent way of fundraising for small groups and societies.

Can you help us with information about any of the Frith photographs in this book?

We are gradually compiling an historical record for each of the photographs in the Frith archive. It is always fascinating to find out the names of the people shown in the pictures, as well as insights into the shops, buildings and other features depicted.

If you recognize anyone in the photographs in this book, or if you have information not already included in the author's caption, do let us know. We would love to hear from you, and will try to publish it in future books or articles.

Our production team

Frith books are produced by a small dedicated team at offices in the converted Grade II listed 18th-century barn at Teffont near Salisbury, illustrated above. Most have worked with the Frith Collection for many years. All have in common one quality: they have a passion for the Frith Collection. The team is constantly expanding, but currently includes:

Jason Buck, John Buck, Heather Crisp, Isobel Hall, Rob Hames, Hazel Heaton, Peter Horne, James Kinnear, Tina Leary, Eliza Sackett, Terence Sackett, Sandra Sanger, Shelley Tolcher, Susanna Walker, Clive Wathen, Jenny Wathen and Douglas Burns.